Deliverance from the Python Spirit.

Powerful Prayers to Overcome the Python Spirit – Spirits of Lies, Deceptions and Oppressions.

DANIEL C. OKPARA

Published By:

Better Life Media.

BETTER LIFE WORLD OUTREACH CENTER.

Website: www.BetterLifeWorld.org

Email: info@betterlifeworld.org

This title and others are available for quantity discounts for sale promotions, gifts and evangelism.

Visit our website or email us to get started.

Any scripture quotation in this book is taken from the King James Version or New International Version, except where stated. Used by permission.

CONTENTS

FREE BONUS ...

Download These 4 Powerful Books Today for

FREE... And Take Your Relationship With

God to a New Level.

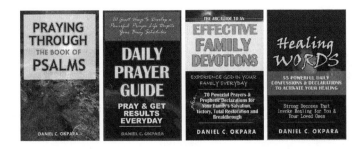

Chapter 1: Understanding the Operation of the Python Spirit.

---

*"It happened that as we were on our way to the place of prayer, we were met by **a slave-girl who had a <u>SPIRIT OF DIVINATION</u>** [that is, a demonic spirit claiming to foretell the future and discover hidden knowledge], and she brought her owners a good profit by fortune-telling"* - Acts 16:16 (AMP).

The original Greek text used in the place of **spirit of divination** in that text is "spirit of python." This spirit's works is to profit from deception, make-believe and lies.

I understand clearly how the spirit of python works because there are many communities in my country, including my village where I come from, that worship python. In those communities it is considered a sacrilege to kill a python. If anyone does kill a python by accident or by intention, the person is required by tradition to bury and mourn the python like a full grown human being for several days. In fact, they believe that if a python comes to your house, it has brought you goodwill. All you have to do is just speak to it and it will peacefully leave. It doesn't harm them...so to say.

However, the Bible makes us understand that

the spirit of python is a deceptive spirit that also works in other ways to subdue its victims.

Here's how the spirit of python works...

1. Deception and Lies

In Genesis, it was this spirit that possessed the serpent to lie to Eve, twisting the Word of God and ultimately worked towards creating enmity between God and man. That's the ultimate goal of the python spirit. It will lie to your mind and create all manner of thoughts against God.

It will try to convince you that God does not really care, otherwise, why would you be going through the kind of problems you are going through. It will remind you how much you have prayed, fasted and sowed seeds and yet have nothing to show for it. It will try to point to you other believers who are suffering and try to get you to reconsider your absolute faith in God.

When you begin to get this kind of dialogue in your mind, recognize that the spirit of python has come to oppress you. Bind it and cast it into abyss, in Jesus name.

2. Divination and Fortune-Telling

There are many people who are possessed with the spirit of python today and use it to practice all manner of prophecy and visions and palm reading. This is why God has warned us not to be drawn away by prophecy but to test every spirit. Notice that in the referenced text above, this same spirit told the truth about who the apostles were. But the ultimate goal is really to make profit and not the salvation and true deliverance of God's people.

In our ministrations, we have come across people whose problems began or became more complicated because they submitted themselves to be prayed for or were laid hands by people who were possessed by the spirit of python. Usually, these people were drawn by the prophecies and visions, but at the end they never got solution to their problems, instead they were used to make profit for the vision giver.

There is no easy way for you to know if you have been a victim of this kind of demonic oppression other than to submit yourself to the LORD and pray for cleansing from any spiritual contamination from the python spirit, directly or indirectly.

3. Spreading Lies About You

The spirit of python is a seducing spirit that twists truths and spread lies. If this spirit has been unleashed against a person, he will be a victim of what I call *lie-share*. All sorts of lies will be manufactured against the person and spread to cause him some kind of hurt.

This is different from people criticizing you for

being good at something. We all face criticism. But this is sheer lies being spread to harm you in your place of work, business, ministry, etc. Sometimes you can't tell where all the lies are coming from. But people are believing and spreading them and locking you out of your entitlements.

Your problem is not the people but the python spirit. You need to buckle up and bind this spirit and cast it into abyss.

4. Demonic Oppression

Another way that the spirit of python operates is by oppressing individuals. As you know, python kills her prey by strangling life out of it. The ultimate goal of the python is to steal, to kill and to destroy (John 10:10). But it begins with suffocating the individual.

There are oppressions that are a result of the spirit of python working against a person. Things like extreme depression, suicide tendencies, life in complete disarray, dizziness and confusion, etc. Quickly recognize these demonic activities and bind the demons and command them to vamoose.

5. Demonic Possession

This demon can also possess people and cause them to live a life of lie. These people will be like they are natural liars. They will be used to cause a lot of harm and frustrate life for others who are in any relationship with them.

Chapter 2: How to Pray for Deliverance from Python Spirits and Release Your Blessings

---

"...I saw Satan fall like lightning from heaven. See, I have given you authority to tread on snakes and scorpions, and over all the power of the enemy. Nothing will harm you. "Nevertheless, do not rejoice that the spirits submit to you, but rejoice that your names are written in heaven."

- (Luke 10:18-20)

Of course, the first step to deliverance from python spirits is to surrender to the

LORDSHIP of Christ and decide to serve God, as a free person. Those who receive Christ as their LORD and savior have their names written in the Book of Life. They can bind and cast out demons and break the power of evil and nothing shall by any means hurt them.

You can bind and cast out the devil and destroy the power of the python from your life and family as a child of God. Yes, you can and should learn to do that. In fact, the book of Proverbs said:

"Deliver thyself as a roe from the hand of the hunter, and as a bird from the hand of the fowler." - **Prov 6:5**

You can and should deliver yourself. No one can pray for you the way you will for yourself. You hold the key into your life. Whatever you forbid will be forbidden, and whatever you allow will be allowed. So here are the steps to minister deliverance to yourself or to a loved one.

1. THE POWER OF WORSHIP

One thing the spirit of python hates is worship to God. It hurts her badly to see people worship God. Several times people possessed with this spirit fall down and begin to wriggle like a snake and confess when we get involved in some serious worship to God.

So the easiest way to deal with this spirit is to

spend a good time and worship God. As you surrender to God in serious worship, you take authority and thread upon this spirit (snakes and scorpions) and then you can rebuke it and command it to flee into abyss.

Deep and power worship scares and defeats the spirit of python, and ultimately, the devil.

2. FAST AND PRAY

Jesus said that there are stubborn demons that will try to resist our prayers, but with fasting we can be adequately prepared to crush them. (Matthew 17:21). Fasting increases the power of prayer several times over.

When you fast, the Holy Spirit will open your

eyes to doorways that need to be removed. It is highly recommended that you fast for 3 days or more and pray these prayers all these days.

There are different kinds of fasting. But whatever kind of fasting you can do, that is okay. I usually encourage people to drink water when they are fasting. Whichever kind of fasting you decide to do, whether it is 6-10am, 6-12:00 noon, 6PM-6AM, that's okay.

3. LOCATE EVERY EVIL DOORWAY AND DEAL WITH IT.

Ask the Holy Spirit to show you what open doors you might have that would allow the python witchcraft spirits to oppress you or come into your life and home. He will show you things and areas that need to be addressed.

Some doorways may be sins, while others may be unknown objects, books, tools, etc. somewhere in the house or property. As you pray, and follow the leading of the Holy Spirit, He'll put it in your heart, areas that you may need to confess sins to the LORD or things to take away and destroy.

Just be open to the Holy Spirit to show you what needs to be done here.

4. PRAY MAINLY IN THE NIGHT

Prayers to deal with python attacks, possession or oppression are better done in the midnight, usually between the hours of 12 midnight to 4AM. Spend a good time in praise and worship and then embark on the prayers here to set yourself free.

Remember, if you ever feel threatened or attacked by python spirits in the future, you can come back to these prayers until you obtain your deliverance

5. ALL THE PRAYERS.

There are about 50 prayer points in the prayer chapters below. They range from confession prayers, declaration prayers, and deliverance prayers, to prayers of intercession for your family. It may not be possible for you to pray all these prayers in one session. You may spread the prayers into 3 or 7 days. You can start where you stopped the previous day.

But I advise that you pray all the prayers for each prayer session and all the entire prayers for this prayer project...breaking the power of witchcraft and releasing buried blessings.

6. PRAY WITH THE WORD.

This book will help you pray with the word of God effectively. Your prayers will have more power and produce more effect when they are saturated with God's Word.

So, in praying the prayers in this book take time to read the scriptures that are recommended and personalize them. If after reading a scripture, you feel like praying some other way before coming back to this outline, that's okay.

7. PRAY WITH AUTHORITY.

Please do not recite the prayer points in this book. That is, do not just read them only and say you have prayed.

The prayer points are just guides. As you read out one, spend time praying it through with words the Holy Spirit puts in your mouth.

Chapter 3: **Prayers to Defeat Python Spirits.**

Once again, bear in mind that as we pray the prayers below, every python spirit connection you have will be destroyed and you will be set free in Jesus name.

SCRIPTURES FOR REFLECTION AND CONFESSION.

Luke 10:19: Behold, I give unto you power to tread on serpents and scorpions, and over all the power of the enemy: and nothing shall by any means hurt you.

Psalm 91:13: You will tread upon the lion and cobra, The young lion and the serpent you will trample down.

Mark 16:18: "They will pick up snakes with their hands, and if they drink any deadly poison, it will not harm them; they will lay their hands on the sick, and they will be made well."

PRAYER 1: TO BIND AND CAST OUT PYTHON SPIRIT.

1.

Heavenly Father, I thank You for giving me power to thread upon snakes and scorpions and nothing will harm me. Thank You for giving me power over the spirit of python, its works, and leader, the devil, through the name of Jesus Christ.

Today, O LORD, as I exercise my authority over this foul spirit of lies and deception, I believe that its works will be terminated in my life and family, in Jesus name.

2.

Father, It is written that in the name of Jesus Christ every knee must bow (Philippians 2:10).

Today, LORD Jesus, I bow before the THEE and submit my will, emotions, heart and everything about me to THEE.

You are the LORD of my life, my family and my destiny.

I accept Your Word for what it is...YEA AND AMEN.

You are not a liar. Whatever You have said about my life is true and must stand.

I reject any other contrary spirit of lies disputing Your WORD in my heart, in Jesus name.

3.

I command to cease this day, all the voices of lies, deception and vainglory, from you spirit of python, in Jesus name.

4.

I disconnect by fire, whatever is serving as a point of contact and connection between me and the python spirit, in Jesus name.

5.

O LORD, let every python egg and instrument in my life and family catch fire right now and be destroyed in Jesus name.

6.

I set myself and my family FREE from the bondage of the python and the devil, in Jesus name.

7.

Let fire from Heaven destroy today, every pythonic venom released against my life, my career, my ministry, my home and marriage, in Jesus name.

8.

Ever man or woman cooperating with the spirit of python against my life and destiny, I command them to be arrested and surrender to the LORDSHIP of Jesus Christ this day, in Jesus name.

9.

O LORD, according to Your WORD, I crush the head of the python and its seeds and trample them to death, forever and ever over my life and family, in Jesus name.

10.

Today O LORD, I decree a total recovery of my health, my wealth and my breakthrough that have been diverted by the serpent before now, in Jesus name.

11.

I set myself and my family free from every kind of spiritual oppression in the dream, in ministry, in marriage and in every aspects of life, in Jesus name.

12.

Every wound inflicted upon my bod by the

serpent and the devil, be perfectly healed this day, in Jesus name.

13.

Every witchcraft serpent sent to attack me and my household, die by fire, in Jesus's name.

14.

From today, I bind every serpent chasing me in my dreams and I command them to die by fire, in Jesus name.

15.

I reverse every curse of shame and disgrace against me and my household. I decree that we shall never be put to shame, in Jesus name.

16.

I decree this day that my body is separated unto the LORD. My body is the temple of the Holy Spirit. I reject every form of spiritual and physical evil defilements from now onwards, in Jesus name.

PRAYER 2: PROPHETIC DECLARATIONS FOR NEUTRALIZING THE SERPENT'S VENOM.

17.

From today, I declare and decree that I am no longer a victim of the spirit of the serpent. I am now trampling the serpent under my feet and crushing its head to death.

18.

I declare and decree that the name of Jesus Christ is the divine rod of the Almighty God. His name shall continually swallow up every satanic serpent that dares to manifest in my presence, from this day forward.

19.

I declare and decree that as I fellowship with God in prayer and Bible study from this day forward, all the effects of the serpent's bite and venom in my life has been totally nullified

---

20.

I declare and decree that by the precious Blood of the Lamb, the Blood of Jesus Christ and the Sword of the Spirit, the serpent will no more have the ability to rear his crushed heart and broken neck to hiss at me again.

21.

My life is soaked and saturated with the Blood of Jesus Christ.

I am sealed with the fire of the Holy Spirit.

I am surrounded by the Glory of the Almighty God.

I am anointed to crush the serpent and the devil every day – in the heavens above, on earth, and in the waters beneath, where I have been empowered to rule and reign as a king in Jesus' Mighty name.

PRAYER 3: **FOR DELIVERANCE FROM UNDESIRABLE, DESTRUCTIVE HABITS AND STRONGHOLDS**

REFLECTION: Romans 12:1-2, Psalm 1:1-3, 2 Corinthians 10: 4-5.

1.

Almighty Father, I surrender my body to YOU this day. I hand over my thoughts to you and dedicate my mind, imagination and attitude to you henceforth, in Jesus name.

2.

O LORD, uproot out of my life every inner

argument and unbelief contesting your Word in my life, in Jesus name.

3.

I hereby arrest every negative thought in me, resisting the move of the Holy Spirit.

I command these thoughts to wither by fire right now, in Jesus name.

4.

Every spiritual stronghold in my life working against the knowledge of God, I pull you down right now, in the name of Jesus Christ.

5.

I command all the false gods contesting for worship in my life, die by fire, in Jesus name.

6.

Every bad habit in my life, causing a barrier between me and the power of God, O LORD, let your fire destroy them this moment, in Jesus name.

7.

From today LORD JESUS, plant in me an

everlasting hatred for every work of the flesh as revealed in Your WORD.

I claim my freedom from every destructive habit.

You spirits of anger, lust, dishonesty, lying, spiritual laziness, pride, exaggeration, alcoholism, smoking, gossiping, and criticizing – by the blood of Jesus Christ, I declare that I am forever free from all of you.

I command you all to leave my life now and go into the abyss in Jesus name.

8.

O LORD my Father, whatever evil effect

happening in my life, resulting from my characters, past mistakes, or addictions to negative thoughts, words and actions, LORD, please set free, in the name of Jesus Christ.

9.

Whatever curse and obstacle my wrong association and friendships have brought upon my life, O LORD, let them be destroyed today, in the name of Jesus Christ.

10.

Father, from now onwards, surround me with the right people; surround me with people who will challenge me towards a Godly and excellent life.

In Jesus name.

I commit myself never to walk in the counsel of the ungodly, nor stand in the way of sinners, nor dine with mockers.

Cause me by Your Spirit to find delight in seeking You and following Godly counsel.

Make me like a tree planted by the riverside that will bear fruit in all seasons.

In Jesus name.

PRAYER 4: RELEASING FAVOR, BREAKTHROUGH AND BLESSINGS

1.

"Heavenly Father, I give You praise because You delight in the prosperity of Your people. I give You praise because YOU supply my needs according to Your riches in Christ Jesus. Receive my praise today in Jesus name."

2.

"How often do I think that prosperity, money and success is by my own efforts and will

alone. LORD, I come to YOU this day and confess my ignorance and pride. Forgive me for not giving YOU the ultimate place in my finances in the past. Forgive me and let Your mercy prevail over me this day, in Jesus name.

3.

By the Blood of Jesus, I receive forgiveness of sins. I receive forgiveness for any form of greed and financial impropriety in the past. LORD Jesus let Your Blood speak for me spiritually from this moment, in Jesus name.

4.

"Thank YOU LORD Jesus because in YOU I have forgiveness of sins. In YOU I have grace to appear before the Almighty God to obtain mercy and find grace in time of need. In YOU I have assurance that when I pray, I receive answers. This is the confidence that I have, that as I pray for my finances this day, I have answers to Your Glory, in Jesus name.

5.

"Almighty Father, as it is written in Your WORD, in Job 36:11, that if I obey and serve YOU, that I will spend my days in prosperity and my years in plenty. LORD, I come to YOU this day and ask for grace to obey YOUR

Word on finances and in every aspect of life,

in Jesus name.

6.

"HOLY SPIRIT, I come to YOU today, I ask You to make me willing and obedient to the WORD of God henceforth according to Isaiah 1:19 so that I may eat the good things of the land. Uproot every seed of greed and disobedience from me this day, in Jesus name.

7.

"Dear LORD, I ask YOU to make me a

blessing in this world, that my life will be a light and support to those who are in need, for it is written that when I give, You will command men to give back to me. Inspire me to give and to give joyfully without regrets from today, in Jesus name.

8.

"Holy Spirit, please motivate me and help me to honor the LORD with my resources and finances from this day, so that my barns will be full and overflowing with harvest, in Jesus name."

9.

"Heavenly Father, I stand in the authority in the name of Jesus Christ right now. I command every demon working against my business, my career and my finances to collapse, be bound and cast into the abyss, in Jesus name.

10.

"It is written in Matthew 16:19 that whatsoever I bind here on earth is bound in heaven and whatsoever I loose here on earth is loosed in heaven. I therefore bind every spirit of poverty, lack, frustration and loss. I cast them into the abyss from today, in Jesus name.

11.

"O LORD, based on Your Word we have authority here on this earth and according to (Mark 11:23) we can speak to the mountain and it will have to obey us. So devil, I speak to you in the name of Jesus Christ, I command you to take your hands off my finances right now in the Name of Jesus.

12.

"I speak to the mountain of Lack and Want, I command you to be removed and cast into the sea from this day, in the Name of Jesus.

13.

"I hereby declare all curses against my life null, void, and destroyed from today. I am redeemed from the curse of poverty! I am free from oppression, in the name of Jesus Christ.

14.

I now loose the abundance of God, and all that rightfully belongs to me now to start locating me, in Jesus name.

15.

I thank You O LORD that You have a plan for me to overcome this have abundance. I cast all my cares and money worries over on You

Lord. I WILL NOT WORRY anymore, neither

will I FRET. I have peace and I'm enjoying

God's supplies, in Jesus name.

16.

"It is written that angels are ministering

spirits sent to minster unto the heirs of

salvation. Therefore LORD, I ask that your

angels of goodness, love and success begin to

minister to my needs henceforth, in the name

of Jesus Christ.

17.

"Wherever my finances are, whoever is

connected to my financial breakthroughs, O LORD, let your angels begin to reconnect them to me this day. As I step out to work on my business or career, LORD Jesus, men and women will bring me favor, in Jesus' name.

17.

Heavenly Father, it is written that You give us power to create wealth. Therefore, I ask You to give me the power, wisdom and guidance to create wealth in my life. In Jesus name.

18.

"LORD, I ask YOU today for ideas, I ask YOU

for inspiration and divine strategies to turn my career around and grow my business into a global brand. Show me secrets hidden from men and help me to unleash YOUR full potential in what I am doing at the moment, in Jesus name.

19.

"O LORD, make me an employer of labor, so that I will be a blessing to others and fulfill the covenant of Abraham which I inherit in Christ Jesus.

Direct me to men and materials that YOU have assigned to bring me into my place of financial and business dominion before the world began, in Jesus name.

20.

"Holy Spirit, You are my teacher. I ask You to teach me how to make profit in my business and career. Teach me to become a shining light in my business and career. Open my eyes to the right job opportunities and profitable business ventures, in Jesus name.

21.

Heavenly Father, I thank YOU for Your Word, in Psalm 1:3, which says that I am like a tree planted by the riverside. Whatever I do prospers. Lord I pray, let your blessing and prosperity fill my house, in Jesus name.

22.

"It is written in 1 Corinthians 9: 8 that God is able to make all grace abound toward me; that I, always having all sufficiency in all things, may abound to every good work.

"Therefore, LORD, I decree that from this day, I have all sufficiency in all things and I lack nothing. I decree that the grace of God is causing me to abound in every good work, in Jesus name.

23.

"It is written in Psalm 112:3 that wealth and riches will be in my house, and his righteousness endures forever.

"So I decree that my house shall be filled with wealth and riches in Jesus name"

24.

"The Lord is my Shepherd. He prepares a table before me in the presence of my enemies. He anoints my head with oil. My cup runs over with blessings!

Money comes to me right now. God is opening the windows of heaven for me. He meets my every need according to His riches in glory by Jesus Christ.

He is causing men to give unto me good measure, pressed down, shaken together and running over, in Jesus name

---

25.

God has given me the power to get wealth. I'm blessed in the field. I am blessed going in and going out. I have the favor of God. Favor, breakthrough, success, money and every good thing comes to me from this day, in Jesus name.

PRAYER 5: MANIFESTING THE FRUIT OF THE HOLY SPIRIT

REFLECTION: - Galatians 5:22-23

1.

Heavenly Father,

Thank You for engrafting me in Christ Jesus by the Holy Spirit as a branch.

You designed me to bear fruits of righteousness, love, peace, joy, gentleness, self-control, goodness, patience, and kindness.

O LORD, I desire to bear these fruits in my life henceforth,

In Jesus name.

2.

Dear Holy Spirit,

I desire to remain rooted in Christ, bearing fruits that lead others to the light of God's love.

I desire to walk in LOVE, forgiving others at all times and gifting God's blessings in my life with others, just as God Loved and gave Jesus to die for us.

I desire to walk in joy every day of my life, thereby drawing from the well of *salvation.*

Please remind and help me at all times to LOVE and be joyful as I live, in Jesus name.

3.

Dear Holy Spirit,

I desire to walk in peace *with myself and with others as a child of God.*

I desire to walk in patience, *for faith makes no haste.*

I desire to walk in kindness, *thoughtfulness and compassion for others just as Christ was compassionate at all times.*

Provide me with daily assistance to bear these fruits of **peace, patience** *and* **kindness** *in abundance, so that Jesus will be glorified in my life every day, in Jesus name.*

4.

Dear Holy Spirit,

I desire to bear the fruit of Goodness, *so that I may lead others to Jesus Christ.*

I desire to be faithful *at all times with whatever God blesses me with, so that I may stand before God in the end and receive the rewards of faithfulness.*

I desire to be gentle *with myself and others, in thoughts, words and actions, so* *that I may be an instrument of encouragement and uplifting to others and not discouragement.*

I desire to walk in Self-control *in food, dressing, and in everything so that I could win the race set before me and not be a cast away after preaching to others.*

I call upon You to empower me every day to bear these fruits as I live, serve God and relate with others.

In Jesus name I pray. Amen.

Chapter 4: **How to Maintain Your Victory Over the Python Spirit.**

"When the unclean spirit has gone out of a person, it passes through waterless places seeking rest, but finds none.

Then it says, 'I will return to my house from which I came.' And when it comes, it finds the house empty, swept, and put in order.

Then it goes and brings with it seven other spirits more evil than itself, and they enter and dwell there, and the last state of that person is worse than the first. So also will it be with this evil generation."

–Matthew 12:43-45

Jesus is simply saying here that there is a probability that one gets delivered from sickness, curses and evil spirit attacks and the problems come back again and the situation become worse than it were in the beginning.

But it doesn't have to be so.

The Word of God gives us an idea of how we can keep our deliverance and victory permanent.

1. Do Not Keep Your Spirit Empty.

From Jesus' statement above, it's obvious that if you leave your spirit empty, you might get attacked with worse situation.

Consequently, it's important to fill your spirit with positive thoughts and vibrations.

Learn to fill your mind with God's Word on a daily basis. The Bible says,

"Keep this Book of the Law always on your lips; meditate on it day and night, so that you

may be careful to do everything written in it. Then you will be prosperous and successful. -
Joshua 1:8"

Work out a system to read the Bible daily, one or two chapters a day and your spirit will have content that will resist the enemy at all times.

2. Serve The Lord.

"So you shall serve the LORD your God, and He will bless your bread and your water. And I will take sickness away from the midst of you. No one shall suffer miscarriage or be barren in your land; I will fulfill the number of your days." – **Exo. 23:25-26:**

Find a place in God's kingdom and do His work. Join in sharing tracts, the prayer team, the ushering department... just get busy for the LORD, and no enemy will have grounds over your life

3. Exercise Your Faith.

It is possible that you experience some form of attack, temptation and setback in your life, from time to time. That doesn't necessarily mean that you are not delivered.

It's important for you to believe that you have been delivered and confess your deliverance, and stop running to and fro looking for other types of prayers for deliverance any more. Remember what the Bible says:

"Now faith is the assurance (title deed, confirmation) of things hoped for (divinely guaranteed), and the evidence of things not seen [the conviction of their reality—faith comprehends as fact what cannot be experienced by the physical senses]. 2 For by this [kind of] faith the [a]men of old gained [divine] approval – Heb. 11:1(AMP).

4. Share Your Testimony.

When you share your story with others, your blessings become permanent. Jesus told the healed man...

"Return to your home, and declare how much God has done for you." And he went away, proclaiming throughout the whole city how much Jesus had done for him - **Luke 8:39 (ESV)**

5. Learn to Maintain A Positive Outlook About Life And Keep Speaking Positive Things About Your Life.

Proverbs 18:21 - Death and life [are] in the power of the tongue: and they that love it shall eat the fruit thereof.

1 Peter 3:10 - For he that will love life, and see good days, let him refrain his tongue from evil, and his lips that they speak no guile:

Ephesians 4:29 - Let no corrupt communication proceed out of your mouth, but that which is good to the use of edifying, that it may minister grace unto the hearers.

God bless you.

Other Books By the Same Author

1. Prayer Retreat: 21 Days Devotional With 500 Powerful Prayers & Declarations to Destroy Stubborn Demonic Problems, Dislodge Every Spiritual Wickedness Against Your Life and Release Your Detained Blessings

2. HEALING PRAYERS & CONFESSIONS: Powerful Daily Meditations, Prayers and Declarations for Total Healing and Divine Health.

3. 200 Violent Prayers for Deliverance, Healing and Financial Breakthrough.

4. Hearing God's Voice in Painful Moments: 21 Days Bible Meditations and Prayers to Bring Comfort, Strength and Healing When Grieving for the Loss of Someone You Love.

5 . Healing Prayers: 30 Powerful Prophetic Prayers that Brings Healing and Empower You to Walk in Divine Health.

6. Healing WORDS: 55 Powerful Daily Confessions & Declarations to Activate Your Healing & Walk in Divine Health: Strong Decrees That Invoke Healing for You & Your Loved Ones

7. Prayers That Break Curses and Spells and Release Favors and Breakthroughs.

8. 7 Days Fasting With 120 Powerful Night Prayers for Personal Deliverance and Breakthrough.

9. 100 Powerful Prayers for Your Teenagers: Powerful Promises and Prayers to Let God Take Control of Your Teenagers & Get Them to Experience Love & Fulfillment

10. How to Pray for Your Children Everyday: + 75 Powerful Prayers & Prophetic Declarations to Use and Pray for Your Children's Salvation, Future, Health, Education, Career, Relationship, Protection, etc

11. How to Pray for Your Family: + 70 Powerful Prayers and Prophetic Declarations for Your Family's Salvation, Healing, Victory, Breakthrough & Total Restoration.

12. Daily Prayer Guide: A Practical Guide to Praying and Getting Results – Learn How to Develop a Powerful Personal Prayer Life

13. Make Him Respect You: 31 Relationship Advice for Women to Make their Men Respect Them.

14. How to Cast Out Demons from Your Home, Office and Property: 100 Powerful Prayers to Cleanse Your Home, Office, Land & Property from Demonic Attacks

15. Praying Through the Book of Psalms: Most Powerful Psalms and Powerful Prayers & Declarations for Every Situation: Birthday, Christmas, Business Ideas, Breakthrough, Deliverance, Healing, Comfort, Exams, Decision Making, Grief, and Many More.

16. STUDENTS' PRAYER BOOK: Powerful Motivation & Guide for Students & Anyone Preparing to Write Exams: Plus 10 Days of Powerful Prayers for Wisdom, Favor, Protection & Success in Studies, Exams & Life.

17. How to Pray and Receive Financial Miracle: Powerful

Prayers for Financial Miracles, Business and Career Breakthrough

18. Prayers to Destroy Witchcraft Attacks Against Your Life & Family and Release Your Blessings

19. Deliverance from Marine Spirits: Powerful Prayers to Overcome Marine Spirits – Spirit Husbands and Spirit Wives – Permanently

20. Deliverance From Python Spirit: Powerful Prayers to Defeat the Python Spirit – Spirit of Lies, Deceptions and Oppression.

21. Anger Management God's Way: Bible Ways to Control Your Emotions, Get Healed of Hurts & Respond to Offenses ...Plus Powerful Daily Prayers to Overcome Bad Anger Permanently

22. How God Speaks to You: An ABC Guide to Hearing the Voice of God & Following His Direction for Your Life

23. Deliverance of the Mind: Powerful Prayers to Deal With Mind Control, Fear, Anxiety, Depression, Anger and Other

Negative Emotions | Gain Clarity & Peace of Mind & Manifest the Blessings of God

24. 26 Most Commonly Asked Questions About Demons: All You Need to Know to Cast Out Demons, Obtain Deliverance for Yourself, For a Loved One or For Your Family

See all at:

www.amazon.com/author/danielokpara

Get in Touch

We love testimonies. We love to hear what God is doing around the world as people draw close to Him in prayer. Please share your story with us.

Also, please consider giving this book a review on Amazon and checking out our other titles at: www.amazon.com/author/danielokpara .

I also invite you to checkout our website at www.BetterLifeWorld.org and consider joining our newsletter, which we send out once in a while with great tips, testimonies and revelations from God's Word for a victorious living.

Feel free to drop us your prayer request. We will join faith with you and God's power will be released in your life and the issue in question.

About The Author.

Daniel Okpara is a husband, father, pastor, businessman and lecturer. He has authored over 50 life transforming books on business, prayer, relationship and victorious living.

He is the president of Better Life World Outreach Centre -www.betterlifeworld.org - a non-denominational evangelism ministry committed to global prayer revival and evangelism.

Through the monthly Better Life Crusades, Better Life Health and Business Breakthrough Seminars and Better Life TV, thousands of lives have been won to the LORD, healed, blessed and restored to a purposeful living.

He holds a Master's Degree in Theology from Cornerstone Christian University and is married to Prophetess Doris Okpara, his prayer warrior, best friend and biggest support in life. They are blessed with two lovely kinds.

Made in the USA
Coppell, TX
15 September 2020